the Prayer Coin

JOURNAL

ELISA MORGAN

"Take this cup from me; yet not my will, but yours be done."
Jesus

(Luke 22:42)

Take This Cup: honest.
Not My Will: abandon.
Two sides of prayer.

The Prayer Coin Journal

© 2018 by Elisa Morgan
Quotations taken from *The Prayer Coin* by Elisa Morgan

Discovery House is affiliated with Our Daily Bread Ministries, Grand Rapids, Michigan.

Requests for permission to quote from this book should be directed to: Permissions Department, Discovery House, P.O. Box 3566, Grand Rapids, MI 49501, or contact us by email at permissionsdept@dhp.org.

All Scripture quotations, unless otherwise indicated, are taken from the Holy Bible, New International Version®, NIV®. Copyright © 1973, 1978, 1984, 2011 by Biblica, Inc.™ Used by permission of Zondervan. All rights reserved worldwide. zondervan.com. The "NIV" and "New International Version" are trademarks registered in the United States Patent and Trademark Office by Biblica, Inc.™

Author is represented by Alive Literary Agency, 7680 Goddard Street, Suite 200, Colorado Springs, CO 80920, www.aliveliterary.com.

Cover design by Connie Gabbert
Interior design by Gayle Raymer

Printed in the United States of America
First printing in 2018

"Take this cup from me; yet not my will, but yours be done."
—Luke 22:42

While praying to his Father in the Garden of Gethsemane, Jesus both requested ("Take this cup") and relinquished ("Not my will"). Jesus prayed both sides of the prayer coin in a single sentence. He could be honest because he knew the Father loved him and would hear him. He could pray with abandon because he loved the Father and trusted his will.

By following Jesus' example, we can pray this way as well.

Prayer is like a two-sided coin, minted in the heat and pressure of life and spent in the bent-knee of practice. On one side is honest: the freedom to be ourselves in relationship with God. On the other side is abandon: the calling to yield to his desires in our lives and in our world. We spend prayer best, like a coin, when we spend it lavishly with the currency of both sides: honest and abandon.

The Prayer Coin Journal is designed to accompany you through your own prayer coin discoveries. Use it often to chronicle your Take This Cup moments, honestly asking God for what you need in your life—or to remove something that pains you. Then, in the same setting, with the same subject, pause to pivot your prayers to the side of abandon as you pray Not My Will about that very request. In many instances, you'll want to repeat the Take This Cup and Not My Will process for the same topic as God leads you to new insights. Consider praying the prayer coin for others as well, using the same two-sided pivoted plea. Be sure to date each entry so you can note your progress—and God's responses that come to you.

May this prayer coin journal guide your own bent-knee practice. As you pray first Take This Cup and then Not My Will, may you discover the intimacy with the Father that Jesus died to provide.

	TAKE THIS CUP
Luke 22:42	"Take this cup from me;
	Honest
	What I want or don't want
	My desire
What it is:	• a vulnerable and unapologetic verbalization of what is truly within me • a bold request launched in a raw expression
What it does:	• brings all of me to God • drags out the "real" in me • helps me recognize my limitations • reveals my hurts so that God can heal • helps me understand the truth about what I really want or don't want so I can own it and decide what I really want • offers the freedom of being known
What it's not:	a sign of faithlessness or doubt or rebellion against the Father
What prayers could be:	• pleas to remove the pain, grief, rejection, injustice, shame, and sacrifices in my life or in the lives of others • requests for what I—or others—want and need or don't want and need • confessions of what I've done or haven't done or admissions of my mistakes and wanderings • expressing my desires and longings • communicating my selfish musings and selfless yearning
Sample prayer topics:	kids, money concerns, marriage, health, jobs, our nation, our church, addictions, woundings

	NOT MY WILL
yet	not my will, but yours be done."
	Abandon
	Not what I want—what God wants
	God's desire
• a pause • a turn in a different direction • a flip of the prayer coin	• a voluntary choice motivated by love to sacrificially surrender • to yield or relinquish my desires • to give myself over without restraint • an ongoing denial of my will for the will of the Father • a giving over of what I long for, what I believe is right and best and good to what God somehow sees—something that is beyond me and my understanding
	• gives strength and power through learned obedience • builds trust • points to resurrection • brings healing • develops intimacy
	forced or demanded; a blind leap of faith or a lobotomized submission
	• pleas for God to work through the pain, grief, rejection, injustice, shame, and sacrifice in my life or in the lives of others • abandon of my requests for what I—or others—want and need or don't want and need • trust in God's forgiveness of my mistakes and wanderings • relinquishment of my desires, longings, and musings
Sample prayer topics:	kids, money concerns, marriage, health, jobs, our nation, our church, addictions, woundings

DATE

_____

_____

_____

_____

_____

_____

_____

_____

_____

_____

_____

_____

_____

_____

_____

_____

_____

_____

_____

_____

_____

_____

_____

_____

_____

Honest prayer unapologetically recognizes human limitations
and boldly *requests help* from the Divine.

NOT MY WILL

DATE

TAKE THIS CUP

DATE

DATE

Dare we pray "not my will"? Might simply speaking
these words somehow prepare us, teach us, even enable us
to pray a *sincere prayer* of abandon?

DATE

God is good enough to love us as we are and yet not leave us this way.

DATE

_____ • • •
DATE

_____

_____

_____

_____

_____

_____

_____

_____

_____

_____

_____

_____

_____

_____

_____

_____

_____

_____

_____

_____

_____

_____

_____

_____

_____

_____

_____

_____

_____

What might we *discover about Jesus*, ourselves, and God if we
pendulum-swung our prayers between Take This Cup and Not My Will?

• •
_____
DATE

_____
_____
_____
_____
_____
_____
_____
_____
_____
_____
_____
_____
_____
_____
_____
_____
_____
_____
_____
_____
_____
_____
_____
_____
_____
_____
_____
_____

Praying the prayer coin aligns us with God so that we are so integrated, so in congruence with his Being, so *intimately connected* that we want nothing other than what he wants.

DATE

DATE _____

_____

_____

_____

_____

_____

_____

_____

_____

_____

_____

_____

_____

_____

_____

_____

_____

_____

_____

_____

_____

_____

_____

_____

_____

_____

_____

_____

_____

We learn from honest what it is we really want.
We fall into the arms *of abandon* in order to receive it.

DATE

God not only knows us and still loves us, *he wants us*. All of us.

DATE

DATE

•   •
_____
DATE

_____
_____
_____
_____
_____
_____
_____
_____
_____
_____
_____
_____
_____
_____
_____
_____
_____
_____
_____
_____
_____
_____
_____
_____
_____
_____
_____
_____
_____

Jesus prayed his prayer coin of honest and abandon,
embracing the intimacy he possessed with the Father and
modeling the intimacy we too can possess.

DATE

Honest prayer makes us better because it drags out *the real* and
presents it freely before the One who can truly free us.

DATE

DATE

NOT MY WILL

DATE

_____

Abandon is a choice, coming from *love that grows* from obedience.

_____
DATE

_____
_____
_____
_____
_____
_____
_____
_____
_____
_____
_____
_____
_____
_____
_____
_____
_____
_____
_____
_____
_____
_____
_____
_____
_____
_____
_____
_____

Jesus *lived* prayer. Like walking, talking, moving, and being, *Jesus prayed.*

NOT MY WILL

DATE

Jesus wrestled mightily with the enemy *while*
surrendering *his will* to his Father.

DATE

Prayer is like a two-sided coin, minted in the heat and pressure
of life and spent in the *bent-knee* of practice.

NOT MY WILL

TAKE THIS CUP

DATE

DATE

For Jesus, prayer was the expression of *his union* with the Trinity.

DATE

Honest comes from trust and trust comes from *being known*.

NOT MY WILL

DATE

DATE

Utter abandon is an exorbitant action, and one that *was necessary* for the work of the cross to be completed.

DATE

The most *pivotal prayer* of Jesus' earthly life began *honest*.

DATE

DATE

NOT MY WILL

DATE

We cling to our self-made safety, terrified to risk embracing
the freedom Jesus holds out for us.

DATE

This two-sided masterpiece of prayer is an invitation
to *the intimacy* Jesus died to provide.

NOT MY WILL

DATE

DATE

DATE

Love is not about our worthiness, our enoughness.
It's about *God's unendingness.*

DATE

_____

_____

_____

_____

_____

_____

_____

_____

_____

_____

_____

_____

_____

_____

_____

_____

_____

_____

_____

_____

_____

_____

_____

_____

_____

It's a lot to consider praying Take This Cup *and* Not My Will.
We tend to slip into one side or the other.

NOT MY WILL

TAKE THIS CUP

DATE

DATE

The prayer coin practice is just that: *a practice.*

DATE

Honest can be *our teacher* if we allow it to do its work.

NOT MY WILL

DATE

DATE

DATE _____

_____
_____
_____
_____
_____
_____
_____
_____
_____
_____
_____
_____
_____
_____
_____
_____
_____
_____
_____
_____
_____
_____
_____
_____
_____
_____
_____
_____
_____

Abandon can be *hard*. In fact, *real abandon* is *usually* hard.
Next to impossible.

DATE

_____

_____

_____

_____

_____

_____

_____

_____

_____

_____

_____

_____

_____

_____

_____

_____

_____

_____

_____

_____

_____

_____

_____

_____

_____

_____

Jesus extends an invitation to enter into *the intimacy* he was destined to die to provide.

DATE

DATE

DATE

Jesus prayed a prayer of absolute abandon because he knew the Father *trusted and loved* him, and he trusted and loved the Father back.

DATE

We want all of Jesus. The honest *and* the abandon.

NOT MY WILL

DATE

• •

DATE

By practicing this prayer daily, our spiritual muscles strengthen, equipping us to embrace the intimacy *God designed* us to enjoy.

DATE

Take This Cup prayer is *honest prayer* that brings all of us to all of God.

DATE

DATE

DATE

Honest is great—essential even. But when I pray *only* honest,
I don't ever allow for what *God* wants.

DATE

In the pivot between honest and abandon, God has a chance
to *work on us* the way he's always wanted to.

DATE

NOT MY WILL

DATE

Our prayer life and our entire relationship with God comes down to *trust*.

DATE

God is love. And our vulnerable God opens himself
to cover our love-fears with himself.

DATE

DATE

NOT MY WILL

· ·
DATE

Jesus is one with the Father, intimately so. His ultimate goal
is that we would be one with the Father just as he is.

DATE

When we are revealed, we can be *healed*.

DATE

DATE

DATE

Abandon is *a journey* of baby steps away from the lies that
shackle us in brokenness and toward the hope of healing.

DATE _____

_____
_____
_____
_____
_____
_____
_____
_____
_____
_____
_____
_____
_____
_____
_____
_____
_____
_____
_____
_____
_____
_____
_____
_____
_____
_____
_____
_____
_____
_____

The unity Jesus desires for his disciples mirrors *the unity* he possesses with the Father.

DATE

DATE

DATE

True submission can never be forced or demanded.

DATE

The prayer coin is all about *intimacy*. Every bit of it.
The honest and the abandon.

DATE

DATE

NOT MY WILL

DATE

Practicing the prayer coin usually *takes time*.

DATE

Honest prayer has the power to *make us better*.
In opening honest, we open to change.

TAKE THIS CUP

DATE

DATE _____

_____
_____
_____
_____
_____
_____
_____
_____
_____
_____
_____
_____
_____
_____
_____
_____
_____
_____
_____
_____
_____
_____
_____
_____
_____
_____
_____
_____
_____
_____
_____
_____

The prayer coin practice teaches us the spiritual discipline
of obedience, which *grows us up*.

DATE

Honest opens us to help. And help that wholly heals
comes from *God alone*.

DATE

_____
_____
_____
_____
_____
_____
_____
_____
_____
_____
_____
_____
_____
_____
_____
_____
_____
_____
_____
_____
_____
_____
_____
_____
_____
_____
_____

Spend the prayer coin lavishly, with the currency of both sides:
honest and abandon.

DATE

Honest *changes us* and honest changes the way we pray.

DATE

Want more of what you've read here?

———

elisamorgan.com

Sign up to receive Elisa's blog posts.

Book Elisa to speak for your event.

Listen to Elisa on discovertheword.org.

———

Follow Elisa
on Facebook and Instagram
@ElisaMorganAuthor
and on Twitter
@elisa_morgan.

Elisa Morgan
Really

Living really ... Really living